MUFFLED SONG

poems by

Maria Castell-Greene

Finishing Line Press
Georgetown, Kentucky

MUFFLED SONG

Copyright © 2016 by Maria Castell-Greene
ISBN 978-1-63534-064-8 First Edition
All rights reserved under International and Pan-American Copyright Conventions. No part of this book may be reproduced in any manner whatsoever without written permission from the publisher, except in the case of brief quotations embodied in critical articles and reviews.

ACKNOWLEDGMENTS

These poems originally appeared in:

The Avocet: On a Neighbor's Roof
JGIM or Journal of General Internal Medicine: Shoulder Song
Serious thanks to both editors for their encouragement.

Also heartfelt thanks to so many teachers at Stanford University Continuing Studies, especially Brittany Perham, Peter Kline, Robin Ekiss, Geri Doran, Rita Mae Reese, Ken Fields, Andrew Grace and Bruce Snider.

Publisher: Leah Maines

Editor: Christen Kincaid

Cover Art: Tara Saathoff/Norada Art

Cover Photo: Hagop's Photography

Author Photo: Dr. Katherine Schlag

Cover Design: Elizabeth Maines

Printed in the USA on acid-free paper.
Order online: www.finishinglinepress.com
   also available on amazon.com

Author inquiries and mail orders:
Finishing Line Press
P. O. Box 1626
Georgetown, Kentucky 40324
U. S. A.

Table of Contents

Our Ordinary Garden 1

It is Beyond Me 3

On a Neighbor's Roof 4

perch 5

Cove 6

Waltz in the Air 7

Layers 8

Pine Cone Ode 9

Pencil Sharpener 10

Shoulder Song 13

Biochemistry 14

Sea Music 15

Out of Sight 16

Ars Poetica 17

Newfangled Landscape 18

Whew! 19

Thanks 20

Chaotic Cadenza 21

Our Ordinary Garden

Shrubberies
keep beetle secrets

oak worms dangle
on single silk threads

trapdoor spider
fashions silk hinges

snail slides
on glisten

tucks violet eggs
underground

in a room furnished
with rusty rocks

tossed up from
layers unlit below

from sandstone
slump on granite

from strata that flex
above warm under-ocean

spill and seep into innermost
wandering bedrock

warmer gets hot gets
red-orange at furnace

edge—but never mind
we're giddy

from entire garden's
tilt & twirl & loop

It Is Beyond Me

Bewildered I begin,
never learn to swim,
dog-paddle with wounded

as well as assailants. Harm
is the mean and I do plenty,
some drown.

Here at the mercy
of something, I glimpse

the might that indulges me.
Athena sent down a chariot for Medea, too,
my sister in crime; I copy her,

give in to its flight,
reins loose, sway with the gallop,
wheels useless this high in the air.

On a Neighbor's Roof

For today October decides on rain.
Rolls out a cloudy quilt, leaves it to hover
On treetops, tucks us in cozy and sane,
Soaks the tilted stage out the window over
My desk. Main character's into his act,
Prince of Drizzle, awfully waterproof,
Crow owns wieldy beak, wears signature black,
Black stands out vivid on rain-colored roof,
Doesn't hop, it's a hardy, pompous gait,
Stops, bows, beak horizontal. I bravo.
Rain-washed red bottlebrush waits, I wait,
Bird-feet wide on shingle for a solo,
Feather-arms make a damp aerial stair
Of the stuff I breathe, barely know is there.

perch
> *"And creation itself. What to do about it?"*
> *Albert Camus*

I go on two legs
to fetch my grandson
at school

sun's fierce

heed knees
how bone ends meet
absurd hinges slide inside skin

oh the flow forward

will second leg
reinvent upright
in time

grandson waits
sun lights my plight

props swing from
oval holes in a frugal pelvis

me in peril on top

COVE

My twin and I squat, slide on our soles, hands steer
down a zigzag cliff-side path,
we land on sand-glitter.
A tiny cove somewhere near La Jolla, enough room
for two to run around waving beach-brown arms.
Evening, sun's turned an orangey color
you can look straight at,
cliffs back us up, waves ruffle and shine,
we slow and kneel, poke at a poor leathery sea thing,
it shrinks from our pity.
Great jellyfish lies nearby, we know they sting.
Bits of its jelly lie around, each glass-clear piece lit
with sun-color throws light on little sandy hills.
Our arms hail the sun, the sun,
the sun slides its golden gift away,
air stays orange for a while.
Someone calls us from on top,
don't remember the climb back up in the dark.

Waltz in the Air
for my twin

Father's Day canvasses
splashed on by three-year-olds

maddening scraps of 'em
linger like crumbs in a pocket

chaos spectacular
avalanche passengers

muteness our camouflage
next time we'll fly to Berlin

waltz under Linden trees
Northern Lights slice the night

mourning doves sail
on a sliver of noon

merciless shimmering
thunderheads boil below

Continent's wide awake moon
peers in our window day-wan

willfully nimble
here we go down again

down with a roar again
bump upon tectonic plate's raucous ride

Layers

Oh Sun
you come round fiery again
as uphill hiker's blunt boots squash last year's leaves
you catch the grid-marked path boot-soles print
toward the flat where lizard chases and swallows two more flies

mole's room you can't touch underneath lizard's run
mole ate a whole breakfast bulb
fat from your handy heat
mole seldom seeks you
does today
shovel paws start a chimney porthole
lizard sets off for another shining fly
hiker grid prints go

oh Sun
sole and soil
fly wings and lizard tongue
mole's dirty lit eyebrows
meet

Pine Cone Ode

I'll bet I love you 'cause I'm defensive too,
        tawny porcupine found under Coulter pines,
tawny when first I picked you up,
                scales bleached so gray

out here standing by the fence for years,
            long and heavy as real porcupine,
      each lovely out-curved scale
          aims hooklike sharp-tip weapons in rows,

      gouge my palm as I lift you,
                thinking, *looks like a poem to me.*
Pull off red mats of bottlebrush stamens fallen in drifts
                    after bees finished off the pollen.

I'm out here for help. Tawny gone, gray OK,
        Towhee good in rust & black & white
            bounces down & down to scratch for breakfast.

Seems you keep secrets out here.
                I want secrets.

Pencil Sharpener

squats,
  early light
    lights its urgently suppliant pose,
    fearless in the morning,
        six mouths wide open. *Let's go. Choose*

one.
  Cord's plugged in.
    Feed me. Hungry for new wood, careless
    of the outcome, sharpener
        keen to chew a dagger-bare point,

so
  may forest
    be broached—not woods full of air I walk
    with mossy mounds and calm
        purple shade all day on wholesome

paths—
  how 'bout an
    inner wilderness, pliant, wet, shut
    up in bone with branches
        ever quick-sliding info like

sap
  rapidly on,
    new stuff roots between scruffy old-growth-
    thickened trunk-like givens
        where Chaos loiters and whispers,

Let's
   dance! Tip chewed
         clean slips easily inside, wanting
         another Chaos waltz,
               and whatever's in there to glide

on.
   I'm hungry!
         Sharpener's blade-spinning motor waits,
         careless of the outcome,
               wet pliant wilderness waits too.

Shoulder Song

I wonder if you've ever waited, almost naked,
meager gown tied behind your neck,

clothes folded on a chair,
underwear underneath,

and stared, and shivered,
at color pictures of organs and bones.

My choice for warmth
and hope is shoulder bones,

clavicle, scapula, humerus
linked together lightly

like a saxophone solo
air shining between the notes.

Of course the drawing isn't right,
the artist has left out soft parts:

skin, muscle, tendons, vessels,
but she did that on purpose,

so I can see, as I unstick my bareness
from paper that crinkles under me,

hop down for a closer look
in bare feet, at the racheted scapula

that hangs on the back and the stick-rib
of clavicle fixes the front,

knobbed-like-a-club humerus
of upper arm, barely socketed for freer action

and then I solo my own fancy rigging:
I'm in the Olympics, Ukrainian maiden

prances, tosses and catches a stick,
long silk ribbons circle in yellow, pink and green.

BIOCHEMISTRY

What's this? Hang out a shingle?
Words got mashed, sent down in a tangle,
Wait with the hammer, spit out the nails,
doubt is smart, given the details:

talk got chewed and swallowed with food.
Rules: *napkin in lap, be good,*
eat, sit still, be quiet—sit straight,
next comes chocolate pudding, wait...

~ ~ ~

ruly manikin rides the carousel,
others spout words, some even yell,
circles her shingle stored in a thimble,
stirs and cooks at home, at table

grapes, yams and kale feed spiral helix,
her chromosomes soak in the colorful mix,
hydrogen, syntax, oxygen kindle,
fiery smolder doesn't dwindle,

~ ~ ~

unruly woman springs from manikin melt
and shingle's singed with spiral helix lilt,
carousel halts, stuck at an angle...
ah, muffled song comes out of the tangle.

Sea Music

I wake & hear a rocking song
   my bonnie lies over the ocean

tall black trees out there stand calm
   my bonnie lies over the sea

the song rolls in from another place
   it's a here-we-go sailor's song

tilting at dawn in wind and cold
   of salty water I'm made

men bend to coil the anchor ropes
   behind us the wake tumbles green

sails accept exuberant air
   we skim on shiny deep

swells rise dear and sad like breaths
   my bonnie lies over the ocean

ah yes it's billow and trough and blow
   oh bring back my bonnie to me

Out of Sight

you blow in on hasty air
like pollen from trees

I catch up

sun center wakes
greed sings
in syncope breaths

hairy sweaty
garden variety parts
serve sliding fire
sweet as mangoes
you go bull goose loony for a bit

then liquid languid
we can hardly walk

Ars Poetica

Zombie-girl doesn't leave footprints,
        her native smarts shifted by fair means or foul
                into a memorabilia box shoved to the back
    of a hard to reach shelf,
she walks and stares all day at living folk...
            watch it, she's scary—

            anyway, happens along something big,
      something like a faery-godmother good with a crowbar,
        pries her up with many an *ouch!* ... sweeping, swapping
    change goes slow ... up out of sullen zombie-numb gloom—

she yawns and stretches with achy moans,
        alas and *tra-la-la* shriek silent and shove
        till she grabs 'em, hangs 'em to wriggle on loopy lines,
air out in HB pencil in hungry spiral notebooks
            on lines end-stopped or enjambed

and hey, dusty native-smarts unfold shameless
        from memorabilia box five anapests to the line,
           unwrap like color-bursts against a black July sky ...

  Wow... now she's out with zero
                numb-zombie-insulation,
      one leg and both arms in the air,
            fistfuls of anaphora spilling,
  lands with an awkward plop
      in what smacks of a metaphor mud-wrestle mystery show

(shovels are in the closet there,
      showers are up the stairs).

Newfangled Landscape

I fall on a rocky ledge
       washed by sage-scented veils
              sent down from the summit—

Something's over.

Lightning pricks at the slope,
       thunder mutters, trembles my platform,
       sage odor fills up the air.

Wonder who's in charge here—

       Saguaro cactus upright like armies,
       a damp bird flickers inside a spiny-arm Cholla clump,

            a grimace suits this electric landscape,

vibrates with the rock.

Whew!

O planet slinger
igniter of sun
stirrer of salty water
stringer of every electron
digger in chaos for symmetry
you stand up acres and acres of trees
wrap us in breathable breeze
crammed with photosynthetic necessity

you play with glacier and snake
fit me up with homeostasis
earthworm with earthquake
I barely keep up with all this fracas
you're awfully big to be my handlebar
thanks that I'm OK so far

Thanks

Your gift of tiny flowers now again
in drifts fly off the side-yard Laurel tree,
filigree the air like a wedding path,
enough to strew in handfuls on a casket—
I step on heaps when I go out for air,
they pelt my hair like white botanical rain,
they ride my shoe-soles back inside, look up
at me from the floor unbroken: yellow center,
white petals, a couple of stamens, each
as big as an ampersand in fourteen font,
and dozens fly off the gate when I leave
by the side path, some dangle in webs,
we bask among surplus gifts: barbed pinecones,
red bottle-brush spindles and purple sage,
we mingle, zipped gift-like inside of time,
rattle and bump along an uneven path.

Chaotic Cadenza

Unruly thump—oh dear—
you pull off the blanket of sleep
you rattle the ribs—waken fear
your drumbeat makes panic and emptiness leap

Lament for the sweet natal song
lub-dub lub-dub—through the night
it rambled iambic so long—
dreadful this daring wearing-out rewrite

It's true there are tools to make you behave
but here is a palpable trend
we need a bravura wave
on death's-bed it won't do to pretend

Maria Castell-Greene lives on the San Francisco Peninsula with her husband. She's a mother of six, grandmother of nine, plus great grandchildren. Recognized for her writing abilities in daily notes about patients during her nursing career, she retired and took up a new vocation. When assigned a poem in a first writing class, found herself smack dab where she wanted to be. This was quite a late start, compared to fellow writers who found their calling young, however now has 18 years of practice & instruction at Stanford Continuing Studies, plus an enduring writing group. Her poems appear in *The Avocet* and in the medical Journal of *General Internal Medicine*.

www.ingramcontent.com/pod-product-compliance
Lightning Source LLC
LaVergne TN
LVHW041524070426
835507LV00012B/1793